•

SANGHARAKSHITA

•

BUDDHISM FOR TODAY - AND TOMORROW

•

WINDHORSE PUBLICATIONS

Published by Windhorse Publications
Unit 1-316 The Custard Factory
Gibb Street
Birmingham
B9 4AA

Printed by The Cromwell Press, Melksham, Wilts.

Design   Lisa Dedman
Cover design   Dhammarati

British Library Cataloguing in Publication Data
A catalogue record for this book is available from the British Library

ISBN 0 904766 83 7

Publishers note: Since this work is intended for a general readership,
Pali and Sanskrit words have been transliterated without the diacritical marks
that would have been appropriate in a work of a more scholarly nature.

•

Contents

Editor's Preface

Brighton Royal Pavilion is an extraordinary monument to one of the more extravagant phases of English history. Built for the notoriously dandyish Prince Regent in 1818, when Brighton was one of England's most fashionable seaside resorts, its domes and cupolas (influenced by Indian styles of architecture), its hand-painted wallpaper and inlaid furniture, reflect the prevailing fashion of the early nineteenth century for things exotic and oriental.

It was this splendid palace that was the venue in 1976 for the introduction to Brighton (now a thriving centre of alternative culture) of another Indian influence: the teaching of the Buddha. The speaker, however, was determined that this influence should go beyond a superficial change in ideological fashion to make a radical difference to the lives of his audience. Buddhism, he swiftly made clear, could provide more than a pleasing touch of the exotic. In fact, it was not exotic at all. The Buddha's teaching came very close to home indeed. It had implications – revolutionary implications – for every aspect of everyday life.

For some members of the audience what Sangharakshita had to say on those four occasions in 1976 would have been completely new. But there were others present who had already had some experience of what he was talking about, because they had already come across the Friends of the Western Buddhist Order (FWBO).

An Englishman by birth, Sangharakshita had returned to England (after many years as a Buddhist monk in India) some ten years earlier, to found the FWBO. From the very beginning he talked, almost audaciously, as though the new movement he envisaged was already in existence. Spiritual communities, he said, would provide an alternative to nuclear family or solitary life. Right Livelihood businesses would give people the option of working with other Buddhists, to bring work firmly into the sphere of Buddhist practice. And Buddhist centres would fulfil the social as well as the spiritual needs of local Buddhists, so that people need not practise in isolation, but could look to one another for friendship and support.

During the FWBO's first ten years, amid the distractions of life in the sixties and seventies, Sangharakshita's vision slowly began to be realized. For those who threw themselves into the first attempts at community living, who engaged in fundraising for and converting the burnt out ruins of buildings that were to become Buddhist centres, who began the first modest enterprises in the name of Right Livelihood, it was perhaps difficult to get a clear perspective on what they were doing. Now, in the series of talks he gave in Brighton, 'Buddhism for Today – and Tomorrow', Sangharakshita spelled it out. They were engaged in the very beginnings of creating what was to be a new society, even a new world.

These talks are no ornate monument to a passing fashion. To begin with, although they are well-crafted, they are neither ornate nor exotic; here we have some very plain speaking. The principles which Sangharakshita outlined in them have endured and the FWBO has become increasingly substantial in the twenty years since the talks were given. The growth of the FWBO is reflected in the international effort which this book represents, with messages whizzing to and fro along the information superhighway between its editor, Mary Jean Moore, who is involved in FWBO San Francisco, and the editorial team at Windhorse Publications here in England.

Throughout the talks Sangharakshita stressed that Buddhism has a great deal to give to Western people today. He focused on four gifts in particular: a method of personal development, a vision of human existence, the nucleus of a new society, and a blueprint for a new world. The previous year, 1975, he put the same thing another way in a poem entitled 'Four Gifts':

I come to you with four gifts.
The first gift is a lotus-flower.
Do you understand?
My second gift is a golden net.
Can you recognize it?
My third gift is a shepherds' round-dance.
Do your feet know how to dance?
My fourth gift is a garden planted in a wilderness.
Could you work there?
I come to you with four gifts.
Dare you accept them?

Vidyadevi
Spoken Word Project
December 1995

ABOUT THE AUTHOR

SANGHARAKSHITA WAS BORN DENNIS LINGWOOD in South London, in 1925. Largely self-educated, he developed an interest in the cultures and philosophies of the East early on, and realized that he was a Buddhist at the age of sixteen.

The Second World War took him, as a conscript, to India, where he stayed on to become the Buddhist monk Sangharakshita ('protected by the spiritual community'). After studying for some years under leading teachers from the major Buddhist traditions, he went on to teach and write extensively. He also played a key part in the revival of Buddhism in India, particularly through his work among the ex-Untouchables.

After twenty years in India, he returned to England to establish the Friends of the Western Buddhist Order (FWBO) in 1967, and the Western Buddhist Order (called Trailokya Bauddha Mahasangha in India) in 1968. A translator between East and West, between the traditional world and the modern, between principles and practices, Sangharakshita's depth of experience and clear thinking have been appreciated throughout the world. He has always particularly emphasized the decisive significance of commitment in the spiritual life, the paramount value of spiritual friendship and community, the link between religion and art, and the need for a 'new society' supportive of spiritual aspirations and ideals.

•

INTRODUCTION

BUDDHISM HAS BEEN KNOWN NOW in Europe and North America for considerably more than a hundred years, and one might have thought that, at least in some quarters, it would have become fairly well known. Unfortunately this is by no means the case. Even after all this time and so much scholarship, it is still relatively unknown and often misunderstood. Some people, for example, still classify Buddhism as one of the various 'religions' of the world – which it is not, if the word 'religion' is taken to mean (as it almost always is) 'religion as revelation' or 'revealed religion'. For other people Buddhism is some sort of exotic oriental cult. For others again, Buddhism is a system of abstract philosophical ideas, quite remote from ordinary life, something in fact that does not impinge on life at any point. Another misunderstanding that used to be very widespread is the view of Buddhism as simply a code of ethics that tells you what you should or should not do – merely a system of rules and prohibitions. Yet others see Buddhism as a form of asceticism – at least, this was the case when I returned to England from India in 1964. In those days, when people came to visit me in the vihara, or small monastery, where I was staying, they were surprised to find that there were no high walls or barbed wire surrounding the building and that everybody could enter freely and talk to whomever they chose. They seemed to expect that we would be completely secluded from the world, and living in perpetual solemn silence (despite the fact that the vihara was in the middle of Hampstead). This used to be quite a prevalent impression of Buddhism then, that it was something negative, repressive, and life-denying.

In addition to these general misunderstandings, many people identify Buddhism with one or another of its specific forms. For example, they encounter the Buddhism of Thailand or the Buddhism of Sri Lanka and think that this, and only this, is Buddhism. Or they come into contact with the colourful and rich tradition of Tibetan Buddhism, and they are carried away by their feelings for lamas, thigh-bone trumpets, thangkas, and all the rest of the Tantric tradition, and think that this is Buddhism – just this and nothing more. Others read books by Japanese masters, start trying to solve koans, and think, 'Zen! Zen is Buddhism. All the other schools, all the other teachings, are not Buddhism at all. Zen is the real thing!' Perhaps the most damaging identification of this kind is to confuse Buddhism with *Nichiren* Buddhism, a sect that is so far from the central Buddhist tradition as to exhibit some of the characteristics of a 'revealed religion', including an infallible book (the *White Lotus Sutra*), a prophet (Nichiren), and an intolerant and dismissive attitude towards other forms of Buddhism. Confusing Buddhism with any one of its specific forms in this way is like identifying an entire oak tree with a single branch or even a single acorn.

In view of such misunderstandings – and I've just touched upon some of the more prominent, popular ones – it is reasonable to say that Buddhism is not really known in the West. Sometimes it is actually dangerous to be slightly acquainted with something, because we tend to overlook the fact that we do not really know it. As Pope puts it, 'A little learning is a dangerous thing.' In some cases, it might be better to have no knowledge at all, better to wipe the slate clean of all our misunderstandings and misinterpretations and make a completely fresh start. And this is the purpose for which the Friends of the Western Buddhist Order (FWBO) was founded in 1967 – to make a completely fresh start at Buddhism.

The FWBO exists, we may say, to identify the absolute essentials of the Buddha's teaching, and to make those essential principles known and relevant to people's lives in the West. Since its founding in 1967, the FWBO has grown steadily. Not only has it become better known, but more and more individuals have committed themselves to the realization of the ideal for which it stands. It is not that when I founded it I had a detailed or precise idea of what we were setting out to do. However, over the years, the FWBO has gradually come to understand its own nature, so to speak. And this may be said to consist in four things the FWBO has to offer, four things which are of the deepest and truest importance to developing individuals in today's world. These are: a method of personal development; a vision of human existence; the nucleus of a new society; and a blueprint for a new world. Here I want to focus on these four things, and through them I will try to present the concentrated essence of Buddhism in a highly practical form especially suited to the needs of Western men and women – needs that, for better or worse, are fast becoming the needs of the whole world.

1

A Method of Personal Development

THIS TITLE RAISES a couple of questions that have to be answered before we consider what this method actually comprises. For a start, what do we mean by personal development; and why should people need it? Why indeed should they need a *method* of personal development?

If we look at the dictionary, we find that 'to develop' means to unfold gradually, just as a flower unfolds, stage by stage, petal by petal, from the bud. To develop means to evolve; it means to pass through a succession of states or stages, each of which is preparatory to the next; it means to expand by a process of growth; it means to change gradually from a lower to a higher state of being. Development is in fact a law of life. In biological terms, for example, it is the principle of evolution. The unicellular organism develops into the multicellular organism, the invertebrate into the vertebrate. Fish develops into reptile, reptile into mammal, and finally the human-like ape becomes the ape-like human. However, this evolutionary process is simply biological and what develops is simply the bodily structure. Only in later stages of the process do we find any signs of self-consciousness, any signs of psychological, as distinct from biological, development.

The whole of this vast, briefly sketched process of development from amoeba to man represents from a bird's-eye perspective the distance that life has travelled so far. Life has certainly come a long way, and it's a fascinating story. But it doesn't end here, with human beings as we at present know them. From here the process can go on – not that it must or it will, but it can. What we may term the 'lower evolution' can be succeeded by a 'higher evolution', which is the process by which human beings as they are become what they can be; the process by which 'natural Man' becomes 'spiritual Man', the process by which unenlightened humanity becomes 'Enlightened Man', or Buddha. It is the process by which Man becomes that which, in a sense – in a deeply metaphysical sense – he (and of course she) always was.

Although the process of the higher evolution coexists with the process of the lower evolution, it is not simply a continuation of it. There are several important differences between the two. In the first place, as already indicated, the higher evolution constitutes not a biological but a psychological, even a spiritual, process. It concerns not the physical structure of the organism, but the mind; and it refers not simply to the processes of reason or the rational faculty, but rather to a whole cluster of mental activities – intelligence, the more refined emotions, creative imagination, and spiritual intuition. The growth of all these mental activities constitutes the higher evolution, which is thus a truly human development.

Essentially the higher evolution is the development of consciousness, but this should not be understood in some abstract, general sense. It is rather the development of the individual consciousness – the development of your consciousness and mine. Human development is a personal development. It is *our* development – not 'our' in the sense of a corporate, collective development, but our development as individuals, or potential individuals, together. We can no longer rely on being carried forward by the surge of the general evolutionary process as on the crest of an enormous wave. In human beings, at least human beings at their best, reflexive consciousness – consciousness of self – has emerged, and henceforth we can evolve only as individuals. This means individually wanting, and not just wanting but deciding, to evolve, and acting appropriately on that volition.

An author who used to be famous but is little read these days, G. Lowes Dickinson, stated the matter clearly and forcibly in his dialogue *A Modern Symposium*: 'Man is in the making, but henceforth he must make himself. To that point Nature has led him out of the primeval slime. She has given him limbs, she has given him brains, she has given him the rudiment of a soul. Now it is for him to make or mar that splendid torso. Let him look no more to her for aid, for it is her will to create one who has the power to create himself. If he fails, she fails: back goes the metal to the pot and the great process begins anew. If he succeeds, he succeeds alone; his fate is in his own hands.'

'His fate is in his own hands': these – if we accept their force – are momentous words indeed, and they challenge us to acknowledge a tremendous responsibility. We have a responsibility for our own life, our own growth, our own happiness. Sometimes that responsibility seems very heavy, even too heavy to bear, and we may be tempted to try to rid ourselves of the weight of it. We may think how comfortable it would be if only we could hand over that responsibility for ourselves to somebody else – maybe to 'God' or Jesus, or else to some fashionable guru figure, or even to some political leader. There are so many figures and agencies and groups who seem willing to relieve us of this intolerable burden. Sometimes we may even try to forget the whole troublesome question. 'Why bother with all this effort?' we may ask ourselves. Why bother with all these methods and practices? Why not just sit back and enjoy life like an ordinary human being and forget about this notion of a 'higher evolution' and personal development?

But, fortunately or unfortunately, once we have reached a certain point, once self-consciousness has begun to emerge, we cannot do that. We cannot set it all aside and forget about it. We want to grow, and we want to grow simply because we are living beings. Every living being wants to fulfil the law of its own nature, which is to develop. We want to actualize our own deepest potential, to become what we really are, to achieve in time what we are in eternity. If we are prevented from doing this, whether by others or by ourselves, we inevitably suffer, because we are going against the law of our own nature. Think how terrible it would be if in a year's time, or five or ten years' time, we were the same people that we are today. Think how terrible it would be if we never changed or grew in any way.

So we want to grow and develop, but we do not always know how. Many of us find ourselves in this situation today. All sorts of factors, external and internal, impede our growth. We are not satisfied with our progress, but we cannot forget all about the idea of growth and change. Caught in the doldrums, we are dissatisfied with ourselves as we are. We would like to be something greater, nobler, more highly developed, but we do not know how to proceed.

At this point we need a method of development. This is the first thing that Buddhism offers, the first thing that the FWBO offers. And this method is meditation. As we have seen, human development is essentially a change from a lower to a higher level of consciousness, and meditation helps us to make this transition. Not that meditation is the only method of developing a higher level of consciousness. Other methods, such as leading an ethical life, participating in symbolic rituals like those found in Tantric practice, and engaging in devotional practices, social service, or the arts, also affect one's level of consciousness. However, these methods work indirectly, in the sense that they have an effect through the physical body and senses – the mind being included as a sense according to Buddhism. Meditation, on the other hand, acts on consciousness directly, and for this reason it can be regarded as the primary method of personal development.

I have referred to the development of consciousness and levels of consciousness. But how do lower and higher states of consciousness differ, and how can we tell them apart? In what way does meditative consciousness differ from ordinary consciousness? The first important difference to mention is that meditative consciousness depends less on the physical senses. Much of the time ordinary human consciousness is sense-oriented. Sense impressions constantly seep in through the eye, ear, and senses of touch, smell, and taste, and these impressions trigger various sensations. Our minds become preoccupied with these sensations, and we do not try to reduce this preoccupation. In meditative consciousness, however, although sense impressions may be present, the mind does not react to them. Sense impressions recede to the periphery of consciousness; in deep meditation they may disappear altogether, as our consciousness is absorbed in the object of concentration and in the experience of the higher state. Sense-consciousness, or awareness of the world of sense objects, fades: sense objects are either perceived dimly or, in very deep states of meditation, not perceived at all.

The second way in which the higher consciousness differs from the lower is that it is more concentrated. This does not involve a forcible fixation of attention but rather a natural flowing together of all one's energies. Usually our energies are divided; they are in conflict. Sometimes they are not available to us at all. This is often why we have very little energy; it is blocked or suppressed. However, in meditation, especially when we have been practising for a while and have attained some degree of success, these blocked or suppressed energies gradually become liberated and are gently guided in the same direction. Thus the higher state of consciousness is a more integrated state. There is no conflict or division, and consequently we experience tremendous energy.

This is not merely physical energy, although physical vitality may be enhanced; it is psychic and emotional energy liberated in the course of the practice of meditation. This experience of liberated energy is intensely pleasurable, and a higher state of consciousness is therefore a state of joy, rapture, bliss – in other words, a state of intense emotional positivity that we hardly, if ever, experience at other times.

We may notice here an interesting fact – that when we are truly happy, we tend not to think more than is necessary. In fact much of our thinking is unnecessary, and amounts very often to no more than needless anxiety. In the higher, meditative consciousness there is no thought of this kind at all. So long as we are thinking discursively, we are not meditating very seriously. To say that there is no thought is not, however, to say that there is no consciousness or awareness; in fact, in the absence of thought, consciousness is clearer, brighter, and more powerful than ever.

So meditative consciousness differs from ordinary human consciousness in that it depends less on the physical senses, it is more concentrated and integrated, it is more alive and blissful, and it is free from discursive thought. In Buddhism this state of higher meditative consciousness is called *dhyana*, sometimes described as a 'superconscious' state, inasmuch as it is a state of intensified consciousness or awareness made up of intensified concentration, energy, and joy.

Furthermore, there is not just one dhyana state accessible to us, but a whole series of such states. Buddhist tradition commonly distinguishes four dhyanas, or four successively higher states; and these can be described in either psychological or metaphorical terms. Psychologically speaking, in the first dhyana we experience a subtle mental activity, concentration, happiness, and joy. In the second dhyana discursive thought dies away, and we experience only concentration, happiness, and joy. In the third there is a further simplification, and we experience concentration and happiness. In the fourth dhyana the comparatively gross experience of happiness gives way to equanimity, so that we simply experience concentration and equanimity.

This psychological description gives us a good idea of what the four dhyanas are like, but there is a traditional metaphorical account of them which may provide a more vivid sense of their nature. Thus, the experience of the first dhyana is said to be like mixing soap powder with water, blending the two until every speck of soap powder is saturated with water and no drop of water is left over. Then, the second dhyana is likened to a lake fed by a subterranean spring; fresh, clear, cool water constantly bubbles up from deep within. The image for the third dhyana is of lotus flowers that grow in the water and remain completely immersed in and permeated by it. And the fourth dhyana is like the experience of a man who takes a cool bath on a very hot day and then, emerging from the bath, wraps himself in a pure white sheet.

These descriptions of the four dhyanas, both psychological and metaphorical, are traditional; there are other ways to describe them. The most useful terms I have come up with out of my own personal experience and reflection are these: integration, inspiration, permeation, and radiation. In the context of personal development and meditation, the integration is primarily psychological; we are integrating the different aspects and functions of the mind itself. And the nature of integration is such that it is achieved not by force or by means of some external bond, but by bringing these aspects and functions into harmony with a common principle or arranging them around a common centre of interest. Meditation works very much in this way. In the preliminary stages of the practice, it involves focusing attention on a particular sense object, either mental or material, such as a mantra or a coloured disc or our own breath.

This psychological integration is twofold. It is, we may say, both horizontal and vertical. Horizontal integration involves the bringing together of the various aspects of our conscious experience. The process of vertical integration, on the other hand, means integrating consciousness with the unconscious, and it is much more difficult to achieve than horizontal integration because the conscious and the unconscious often pull in opposite directions. However, given a common direction and purpose, they may be brought together. Energy begins to flow from the unconscious into the conscious mind, and concentration then becomes easier. We find that we can meditate: that is, we experience a sense of harmony and repose and an absence of conflict.

Next comes the stage of inspiration. This term derives from a word meaning 'to breathe' – hence, inspiration is what is 'breathed' into us from outside our ordinary, conscious, everyday self. It comes from the heights or, if you prefer, from the depths. It comes, anyway, from some other level of consciousness. Usually we experience this inspiration as an impersonal force or energy – but we may sometimes experience it as a person. The poets, for example, speak of being 'visited by the muse' – a personification of the forces of poetic inspiration – and in ancient times, the poet regularly invoked the muse or goddess of poetry at the beginning of a poem, thus symbolically opening himself to the spiritual energies the muse represented. It is true that in later times the invocation of the muse became a lifeless literary convention, but originally it was an overwhelming emotional and spiritual experience.

This inspirational power is experienced not only by poets. Prophets, for example, find in it a specifically religious force when it arrives in the guise of 'the voice of God', directing their actions and endeavours. As for Buddhists, it may be said to come to them in the form of *nagas*. These are depicted, in the literature and art of the Mahayana tradition, as serpent-like beings with human heads or as human figures with serpentine hoods. They are said to live in rivers, streams, and oceans.

If the nagas represent the forces of inspiration welling up from the depths, the figure of the *dakini* from the Tantric Buddhist tradition represents a corresponding force of inspiration from the heights. *Dakini* is sometimes translated as 'space-traveller' or 'sky-walker'. Buddhist art and temple paintings depict dakinis as beautiful young women flying through the air, trailing rainbow scarves. They symbolize the active forces of higher inspiration moving freely in the vast expanse of reality.

When experienced as rising from the depths, the forces of inspiration seem to bring us up with them; when experienced as descending from the heights, they seem to bend down and catch us up to their exalted level. In either case the experience is the same – we are lifted to a higher level. We are borne on the crest of a wave, or carried on the back of a winged horse; we are taken over by something more powerful than ourselves. Or rather, this is the way it *seems*, for this something is still of course part of ourselves; it is, if you like, another dimension of ourselves. So inspiration is an important stage of personal development. It is intensely pleasurable, even ecstatic. We feel energetic and do everything effortlessly and spontaneously. In fact we may not feel as if we are doing anything at all – things just seem to happen of themselves, in their own beautiful way.

These stages of integration and inspiration can be experienced fairly easily. Most people will experience them after only a few months of meditation, which is why I have gone into them in detail. Since the remaining stages are more difficult to achieve, I will deal with them more briefly.

We can describe the next stage, the stage of permeation, by contrasting it with the previous stage. In the stage of inspiration we experience on the one hand horizontal and vertical integration from the previous stage, and on the other hand a higher level of consciousness which flows into that lower level and is experienced as inspiration. The higher consciousness gradually penetrates the lower consciousness and in the end permeates it completely. The higher level of consciousness also permeates the actual world. We experience that higher level of consciousness not only within ourselves but also as outside ourselves, completely filling the world. The higher state of consciousness is in us, but also we are in it. We are like a balloon which is both filled with air and floating in the air. The same element, the same consciousness, is both inside and out, and there is just a thin transparent layer – which represents one's particular sense of self – between the two.

The fourth and last stage – the stage of radiation – is radically different from the three previous stages. The first three dhyanas are self-contained and inward-looking; they represent the mind's own experience of itself. In the fourth dhyana, the stage of radiation, however, the mind is directed outwards. It is not affected by the world of external reality but instead acts upon the world. In this stage consciousness is highly integrated, positive, and powerful. We could say it is surrounded by an aura that protects it from external influences. At the same time this aura acts as the medium for influencing the outside world. It is rather like an electric bulb: the bulb's glass protects the filament but at the same time the bulb radiates light.

The quality of this radiation is said to be the basis for developing psychic or supernormal powers. In Sanskrit, the word for psychic powers is *riddhi,* which originally referred to the idea of potency, the power to affect one's surroundings. The riddhi of the king, for example, resided in his power of life and death over thousands of people. The riddhi arising out of one's state of consciousness in the stage of radiation works in a completely different way from that of a king, but it too is so powerful that one can affect things without being affected oneself. Some of these effects may well seem miraculous: one can give strength to the weak, overcome hatred with love, and even awaken those who are spiritually dead.

Having defined these four successively higher levels of consciousness, let us look briefly at how we can achieve them. Simply to say that they can be achieved through meditation is not enough. You can't just meditate; in a sense, there is no such thing as meditation. There are only *methods* of meditation, of which Buddhism teaches a rich variety, some common to all schools of Buddhism and others special to particular traditions. Some are especially effective for people of a specific temperament; others work best for people wishing to develop certain qualities or to overcome particular weaknesses.

Take, for example, the method of meditation called in the ancient language of Pali the *metta bhavana. Metta* means 'friendliness' – though in a much more positive, powerful sense than the word possesses in English – while *bhavana* means 'making to be', thus 'bringing into existence' or 'development'. Put together, the two terms translate as 'the development of universal friendliness'. The metta bhavana is therefore meant especially for those who wish to attain higher levels of consciousness by overcoming hatred and developing friendliness. It is undoubtedly one of the most important and effective methods of personal development. At the same time it shares something fundamental in common with all other methods of meditation, in that it works on the basis of one supremely important fact – that we can change. Consciousness can be restructured; negative states like hatred can be converted to positive states like love. And this is one of the strengths of Buddhism; it does not merely exhort you to change, but shows you exactly *how* to change. It doesn't merely urge you to love your neighbour – such exhortation is easy – but it shows you further exactly how to go about this. Moral exhortations are not enough; we need practical help. Unless we are given some idea of how to go about changing ourselves, we simply feel frustrated and resentful. We may even wonder if personal development is possible at all.

Usually the metta bhavana is practised in five successive stages. First of all you develop friendliness towards yourself, because that's where friendliness starts. If you are unhappy with yourself or do not like yourself, you can't really like other people. Love must begin with self-love. Charity really does begin at home, and home begins with you. Then, once you have developed goodwill towards yourself, you extend it outwards, starting with a near and dear friend – someone you know well and care about deeply. The person should preferably be around your own age, and should be someone to whom you are not sexually attracted, since this feeling of friendliness is not erotic. The friend should also be alive; otherwise, the feeling of metta may be tinged with sadness or regret. Next, you bring to mind a 'neutral person' – someone you know quite well by sight and have perhaps met a few times but for whom you have no particular feeling, neither liking them nor disliking them. You then try to extend the same feeling that you have cultivated towards yourself and your close friend to this neutral person. Fourthly, you extend this goodwill to someone whom you positively dislike, or even hate. With a little practice, by the time you come to this fourth stage, you may have developed such a momentum of goodwill that it is quite easy to feel warm towards that person. Feelings of hatred, antagonism, and enmity begin to dissolve; you may feel like letting bygones be bygones and starting afresh. The next time you meet that person you may even be able to feel and behave completely differently, and so begin a new chapter in your relationship.

In the last stage of the metta bhavana you think of all four people – self, friend, neutral person, and enemy – simultaneously, and cultivate the same love, the same goodwill, the same friendliness, towards all four. Then you extend that goodwill in ever-widening circles to everybody in the building where you are sitting, then to all the people in the neighbourhood, then to all the people in the town, and all the inhabitants of the whole country. Moving on, you include all the populations of your continent, and finally you extend your metta to the entire world. One way of doing this is to think of anyone you know in different countries throughout the world, and develop this stage of the practice from there.

Of course, you don't have to think of just human beings. You can think of animals, birds, and fish; you may even follow the ubiquitous Buddhist tradition of cultivating metta towards beings of whatever kind throughout the furthest corners of the universe. In this way the practice concludes. By this point one should feel, at least for a time, a sense of expansiveness, a sense of warmth, goodwill, friendliness, and love that has displaced, or even transformed, other more negative and destructive feelings. This has certainly been the experience of the millions of people over the centuries who have practised this meditation. It has been found to work, and it still works today.

The metta bhavana does not, as a practice, stand alone. It is one of four practices known as the 'four limitless states', so called because you try to develop the appropriate emotion with no limit whatsoever. The other three practices comprise the development, respectively, of compassion, sympathetic joy, and equanimity. But although there are specific practices for their development, these positive emotions cannot really be separated from the metta bhavana. Metta is in fact the basis for them all. When our friendliness comes into contact with suffering, compassion arises. When it comes into contact with other people's happiness, sympathetic joy develops. And when we establish friendliness, compassion, and sympathetic joy equally towards all, then equanimity, or peace, arises. Furthermore, we may add a fifth 'limitless state' to the traditional four: when our friendliness is directed upwards towards a spiritual ideal, we experience reverence or devotion.

These five emotions – friendliness, compassion, sympathetic joy, equanimity, and devotion – are the principal positive emotions that Buddhism encourages us to develop. These emotions occupy a central place in the spiritual life, and when fully developed they constitute what is known as the 'liberation of the heart'. In today's world the development of positive emotion is more important than ever before; without positivity there is no spiritual life. Unfortunately many people in the West fail to realize this. They think religion is dull and gloomy – well, perhaps it is, but Buddhism isn't, and personal development certainly isn't. I would go so far as to say that without strong positive emotion no spiritual progress is possible at all. This means that many people's first duty, to themselves and to others, is simply to be happy: to develop friendliness, compassion, sympathetic joy, equanimity, and devotion.

All this is not, however, enough. There are essentially two different kinds of Buddhist meditation, and up to this point we have touched on only one of them. Meditation as I have described it so far is to do with development of calm – with the calming down of negative, 'unskilful' mental states, and the development of skilful states to the highest possible degree. Although this represents a very high attainment indeed, it has definite limitations. It can be gained, yes, but it can also be lost – and regained, and again lost. For this attainment to be permanent we need to have recourse to the second and, in a sense, higher kind of meditation: the development of 'Insight'.

By Insight with a capital 'I' is meant direct vision, direct experience of the true nature of existence. Here one sees the world as it is. One sees also what is beyond the world – one sees *that* as it is too. One sees the world, the conditioned, the phenomenal, as unsatisfactory, impermanent, unreal, and not ultimately beautiful; and one sees what is beyond the world – the unconditioned – as blissful, permanent, real, and beautiful. Seeing in this way, one finally turns away from the world, away from the conditioned, and turns irrevocably towards the unconditioned. One turns right round. One experiences what is termed in the *Lankavatara Sutra* a 'turning about in the deepest seat of consciousness'. Thus Insight goes beyond 'calm'. It is not, however, independent of it. It is only on the basis of 'calm' that Insight is properly developed. It is because it has behind it the purified and refined energy of the whole being that Insight can penetrate into the depths of existence. Insight is therefore not just intellectual understanding, although the content of insight can often be expressed in intellectual terms, at least up to a point. Insight is direct spiritual vision, direct experience of ultimate reality. And when it is fully developed, one achieves what is called 'liberation by wisdom'. Together, liberation of the heart and liberation by wisdom constitute Perfect Enlightenment.

Calm and insight are both necessary. The purified heart must be united with the illumined mind; love and compassion must be united with wisdom. And when we succeed in this union, our personal development will be complete. When, through this method of personal development, we have achieved this unity, we shall begin to see the world and human existence very differently. Indeed, we shall begin to see as a Buddha sees. It is this vison which I now want to consider.

2

A Vision of Human Existence

Up to this point we have been concerned with the most practical means of self-development available to us. I want now to consider things from a more theoretical point of view. The theoretical, however, can be practical in its own way. There are always going to be people for whom the practical on its own is not, 'practically' speaking, ever going to be enough.

There are several Buddhist classifications of temperament or psychological type. One of the oldest and most basic of these is the simple classification of the followers of the Buddha as being either 'faith followers' or 'doctrine followers'. As the name suggests, faith followers are guided primarily by their emotions, and they usually respond quickly to what moves them. When faith followers hear about meditation, they may well take up the practice without further ado simply because it appeals to them. They don't ask a lot of questions, they don't want to know the whys and wherefores of it all. Often faith followers are also attracted to meditation by the person teaching the meditation, because they attach great importance not only to feelings but also to people, to whom they are drawn by an instinctive positive regard.

Doctrine followers, on the other hand, are guided more by thought, reflection, even prolonged and detailed consideration. They are unlikely to take up a particular practice until they have understood quite thoroughly what it is all about – how it works, and even why it works. In the case of meditation, they will want to know the philosophy behind the practice before they begin, and they will want this philosophy to give them a reason for practising.

The consideration of meditation is perhaps of special interest to the faith follower. What follows will appeal more to the doctrine follower. But inasmuch as most of us are more or less a mixture of the two temperaments, sometimes one predominating, sometimes the other, all of us will find its approach useful at times. At any event, the second great thing that the FWBO has to offer is concerned in some sense – a provisional sense – with philosophy. In the end our subject is not really to do with philosophy at all. It is not a philosophy of existence but a *vision* of existence.

In fact – surprising as it may seem – in the Buddhist tradition there is no such thing as philosophy. In the languages of the Indian Buddhist scriptures, there is no word corresponding to philosophy, either literally or metaphorically. The Sanskrit word *darshana* is sometimes translated 'philosophy', but it actually means 'that which is seen' – a sight, view, perspective, or vision. The word 'philosophy' may literally mean 'love of wisdom', but it is more generally understood to mean a system of abstract ideas; it suggests something thought rather than seen. But *darshana* refers to direct experience and perception – that is, something not mediated by concepts at all.

For example, the *sat darshana* of Hinduism, usually and erroneously rendered as 'the six systems of Hindu philosophy', represent not six systems of abstract ideas, but six ways of looking at existence. The *sat darshana* are, we may say, six sights, six views, perspectives, or even visions. The mode of expression in both Hinduism and Buddhism may be conceptual – it very often is – but the content of the expression is not conceptual at all. The content is a direct perception of things, a vision. But in fact, the Buddhist term is a different one, though it comes from the same root, meaning 'to see'. In Buddhism we use the term *drishti*, which also means a sight, perspective, vision, or view.

Traditionally Buddhism distinguishes two kinds of view: wrong view and Right view. We may understand in general terms the difference between the two kinds of 'philosophical' view or vision by making a simple analogy with ordinary physical vision. With good vision we see clearly and for a great distance. Good vision is unblinkered: we can see all around us. Good vision is also undistorted; nothing clouds or colours or refracts it. Conversely, poor vision may be weak in that we do not see very far or distinctly; it may be blinkered, restricted to a narrow field so that we see only what is straight in front of us; or it may be distorted, as when we look through a thick fog or through coloured glass or bottle-glass.

Wrong view is very much like poor vision. First of all, it is weak. Our mental vision is weak when it lacks the concentrated energy to be derived from meditation. It is this energy that transforms a purely conceptual understanding of the truth into direct experience. If this energy is not there, then we do not see deeply into the true nature of things. We do not see things clearly or distinctly; we do not see them as they truly are.

Secondly, wrong view is blinkered. It is limited to a narrow range of experience, to what can be experienced through the five physical senses and the rational mind. It is to have just this narrow viewpoint from which to draw conclusions, to be simply unaware of other possibilities of perception or experience. On a very basic level this kind of wrong view is exemplified by the poverty of outlook of someone who is interested only in their job, their family, football pools, and television programmes. Having no interest in world affairs, the arts and sciences, or personal development, they see life simply in terms of their own limited existence.

Thirdly, wrong view is distorted. Vision can be distorted by our mood – whether we are feeling happy or gloomy. It can be distorted by our likes and dislikes. If we dislike someone we see all sorts of faults, whereas if we like someone we may see in them all sorts of perfections that they do not really possess. Our vision may be distorted, too, by prejudices regarding race, class, religion, or nationality. Thus wrong view is weak, limited to a narrow range of experience, and distorted by personal feelings and prejudices.

Right view, obviously, is the opposite of this. Right view is powerful. Based on the concentrated energy of meditation, it gives rise not just to conceptual understanding but also to direct experience of the truth. For this reason, it does not remain on the surface, but penetrates deep into the heart of things, and sees everything clearly and distinctly. Secondly, Right view is unlimited. It ranges over the whole field of human experience; it is not confined to what can be experienced through the physical senses or the rational mind. If it generalizes at all, those generalizations are made from the entire range of human experience in all fields, at all levels. Lastly, Right view is not distorted by emotion or prejudice; it sees things as they are.

The distinction between wrong view and Right view is of supreme importance in Buddhism. A view does not, after all, exist in the abstract, somehow apart from people. It belongs to someone. So if we can identify two kinds of view, we may also identify two kinds of people. People whose view of existence is limited, restricted, and distorted are known in Buddhism as *prithagjanas* – the 'many-folk' – and as the name implies, they constitute the majority of people. Most people have not worked to develop themselves at all and consequently are just as nature made them, so to speak. On the other hand, there are those whose view is unlimited in extent, unrestricted in scope, and without any distortion whatsoever. These are known as *aryas*, the 'spiritually noble'. Such individuals, having worked to attain some degree of personal development, have remodelled themselves, at least to some extent. Of course, the crucial point about these categories is that it is possible to move from the one to the other – by developing awareness, by cultivating positive emotions, by raising the level of consciousness, and, above all, by discarding wrong views and developing right ones.

So these two – wrong view and Right view – are what we have to work with, practically speaking. However, there is actually a third kind of view – Perfect View, or rather Perfect Vision. Perfect Vision is Right view developed to the fullest possible extent. It is the total vision of the total man at the highest conceivable level of his development. It is the unconditioned vision of the unconditioned reality. It is the vision that does not just look beyond space and time but is totally unconditioned by it, that totally transcends the ordinary framework of perception. Perfect Vision is the vision of the Enlightened One, the Buddha, the one who sees with wisdom and compassion.

For the most part, our own view is wrong view. Moreover, we tend to rationalize our wrong views, presenting them in systematic conceptual form. These rationalizations are the worldly philosophies, the various -isms and -ologies. Only occasionally do we have a flash of Right view – and such sparks of Right view derive ultimately from Perfect Vision. They become available to us through the Perfect Vision of the Buddha. If we can attend to what the Buddha has communicated of his vision of existence, we can momentarily rise to that level, at least in imagination, and see exactly where we stand. We will have a true philosophy that will enable us to understand the general principles that underlie the whole process of personal development, and that will give meaning and purpose to our lives.

When we look for the source of the Buddha's vision we naturally arrive at a very familiar image – that of the Buddha beneath the bodhi tree 2,500 years ago. He has just attained Enlightenment. He has seen his great vision of human existence, which is in a sense identical with the experience of Enlightenment itself, and which he is afterwards never to lose. But no sooner has he seen this great vision than a problem arises. How is he to communicate that vision? According to tradition – and here we touch upon something very profound and mysterious indeed – the Buddha feels at first that the vision he has seen, the Enlightenment he has attained, cannot be communicated. Sitting under the bodhi tree, he reflects that Enlightenment is, of its very nature, incommunicable. And seeing this – that what he has experienced is very deep, very subtle, very sublime – he sees also how much people are enmeshed in sensual pleasures, how weak, restricted, and distorted is their view, and he feels that it will be impossible for them to understand his vision.

At this point – again according to the tradition, or, if you like, the legend – the god Brahma, the Lord of a Thousand Worlds, intervenes in dramatic fashion. He points out that for want of the Buddha's vision, the world will perish: 'Let my Lord the Exalted One teach the Truth. For there are some beings whose sight is but little clouded with dust. They are perishing through not hearing the Truth.' (The expression finds an interesting echo in the Old Testament: 'Where there is no vision the people perish.') The Buddha then looks out over the world with his spiritual eye. He sees that people are in different stages of development and that some are indeed sufficiently free of the dust of the world to be able to understand.

Having decided to teach and communicate his vision, the Buddha goes about it in various ways. First of all he communicates through concepts – that is, by means of abstract ideas, which is perhaps the commonest means of communication, especially today. Secondly he communicates in terms of myths and parables, metaphors and similes – that is, he communicates through the imagination. Thirdly he communicates through his actions. There is the kind of action that forms the basis of a whole *sutta*, as when he tends a sick monk who has been neglected by the rest of the Order, or when he remains totally unruffled in the face of a rogue elephant deliberately released into his path; or when, to take an example from the Zen tradition, he goes to address the whole Order of monks and simply holds up a flower. There is also the example of the ordinary day-to-day actions through which he communicates. Even when he does nothing but walk along the road, he communicates to anyone who is ready for the communication, just by the way he walks.

Such non-verbal teaching is not confined to Buddhism. There is, for example, a story from the eighteenth century about a certain spiritual seeker who went to see a great rabbi. Afterwards he was asked why he had gone. Was he in search of some great truth or teaching, some explanation of the cabbala perhaps? 'No,' the spiritual seeker said, 'I went to see the rabbi to see how he tied his shoe laces.' Similarly one might go to see how the Buddha wore his robe or how he ate his food. Everything he did would communicate his vision in some way to the receptive aspirant.

Fourthly, the Buddha communicates by silence – by doing and saying nothing at all. He just is. He communicates by his mere presence – which is, of course, a non-presence. Or rather, we should say that he communicates (so to speak) neither his presence, nor his non-presence, nor both his presence and non-presence, nor neither his presence nor non-presence. And if there is one thing that this language of the Perfection of Wisdom tradition makes crystal clear, it is that this type of communication is intensely difficult to receive – if only because we won't simply listen. Before we can receive that silent communication, we have to stop speaking and thinking, even stop, in a sense, being ourselves. As we go on to examine the substance of the Buddha's more accessible communication – through concepts and through symbols – we need to bear in mind his communication through action and through silence. We should not forget that the Buddha's vision is necessarily expressed in action, and that it is a *vision*, a direct, essentially incommunicable experience.

Let's go back now to the figure of the Buddha seated beneath the bodhi tree. As he sat there, he saw that everything was constantly changing, on all levels, on the mental plane as well as on the material plane. It was true of all forms of life. Nothing remained the same, everything was pure process, everything flowed. In terms of Indian thought the Buddha saw that in reality there was no such thing as 'being' or 'non-being', only a vast 'becoming'. But he saw more than this. He not only saw the truth of change – that things arise and then pass away. He also saw that this change was not accidental. Things do not arise and pass away by chance. Whatever arises, arises in dependence on conditions; whatever ceases, ceases because those conditions cease; and the conditions are, as we would say, purely natural conditions. They do not depend on anything like, say, the 'will of God'. Thus the Buddha saw not only the truth of change but also the law of conditionality. Though this law is the fundamental principle of Buddhist thought, it can be stated very simply as follows: 'A being present, B arises. In the absence of A, B does not arise.'

On a certain occasion, Ashvajit, who was one of the Buddha's first five disciples, proclaimed this law to Shariputra, then a wandering ascetic, with immediate results. At the time Shariputra was looking for a teacher, and in his wanderings he met Ashvajit, who was also a wanderer. Impressed by Ashvajit's calm, happy, radiant demeanour, Shariputra asked the standard questions that wanderers used to address to each other: 'Who is your teacher?' and 'What teaching does your teacher profess?' Ashvajit said, 'I am only a beginner. I don't know very much. But what I do know, I shall tell you,' and he thereupon recited the following verse:

Of those things which proceed from a cause
The Tathagata has explained the origin.
Their cessation too, he has explained.
This is the doctrine of the great ascetic.

With one possible exception, this verse is the most famous in all the Buddhist scriptures. Often regarded as a summary of the Dharma (or teaching of the Buddha), it is to be found engraved on ancient monuments and seals throughout the Buddhist world. On hearing this verse, Shariputra grasped and accepted the concept of conditionality sufficiently deeply to set him at once on an irreversible course towards Enlightenment.

Having seen this universal law of conditionality, the Buddha went on to discover something crucial to human development. Conditionality is not all of the same kind. There are two main orders of conditionality at work in the universe and in human life: cyclical conditionality and spiral conditionality. In the cyclical order of conditionality there is a process of action and reaction between pairs of opposites. Pleasure and pain, happiness and misery, loss and gain – and, within the wider context of a series of lifetimes, birth and death – endlessly succeed one another, as if our experience of the world were a kind of pendulum. In the spiral order, on the other hand, factors progressively augment rather than counteract each other. For example, in dependence upon pleasure arises not pain but happiness; in dependence upon happiness arises not unhappiness but joy. It goes on: in dependence upon joy arises delight, then bliss, then rapture, then ecstasy.

In the life of the individual human being, these two orders of conditionality are reflected in two different ways in which the mind may function. We may function from the reactive mind or from the creative mind. If we function reactively, we are not *acting* at all, only *re*-acting.

When we react, we are essentially passive; we are responding automatically to stimuli. To function creatively, on the other hand, means to originate, to bring into existence something that was not there before, whether what we create is a work of art or a higher state of consciousness. It means to act in the full sense of the word. To function reactively is to function mechanically, whereas the creative mind is both spontaneous and aware. When we are reactive we go on repeating ourselves, going over the same old patterns, doing today what we did yesterday, doing this year what we did last year, doing this decade what we did last decade, and even – to extend the context – doing in this life exactly what we did in all our previous lives. However, when we are creative, we change: we move on, we become aware of our old habits of mind and our fixed patterns of feeling and behaviour, and we become free of them.

Personal development therefore is based on conditionality: we cease to live reactively and learn to live creatively. This is by no means easy. It requires, above all, awareness, and awareness in particular of the two kinds of conditionality, not simply as abstract principles but as concrete alternatives actually confronting us virtually every minute of the day. Suppose for example that someone speaks unkindly to us. We can either react by becoming angry and feeling hurt, or we can try to sympathize, to understand what has happened and why, or at least to be patient. If we react, we will be going nowhere except in the direction of reinforcing negative patterns of behaviour; but if we are creative, we at once begin to break down that cycle, and in doing so, we take a step forward in our personal development.

There is of course much more one could say about the Buddha's vision as communicated in conceptual terms, but my intention here is to offer just a glimpse – a partial glimpse – of that vision. We must now move on to do the same with respect to the language of myth and imagery and symbolism – a mode of communication that reached its fullest expression within the Tibetan tradition, from which the following imagery is taken. If we go back to the figure seated beneath the bodhi tree and ask again 'What did the Buddha see?' we may say that he saw two things.

The first thing he saw was a great wheel, embracing the whole of conditioned existence. This wheel contains all living things and is constantly turning. It turns by day and by night, it turns through life after life, it turns with age after age. It is coterminous with the cosmos. We cannot see when it first began turning and as yet we cannot see when it will cease to turn.

This great wheel revolves on a hub made up of three creatures that form a circle by each biting the tail of the one in front. A red cock, greedily scratching the earth, bites the tail of a green serpent, its red eyes glaring with anger. The serpent in turn bites the tail of a black pig wallowing in its own ignorance. Surrounding the hub, which forms the first circle of the wheel, is a second, larger circle divided vertically into two halves and containing figures of men and women. On the left half, which is white, figures are ascending, almost floating upwards, as though to the sound of music. Some are holding hands and all are gazing upwards to the zenith with rapt, blissful expressions. On the right the figures are descending – or rather, they are plunging headlong. Some are naked and deformed, others are chained together, and still others are holding their hands to their heads. All are anguished and terrified.

The next circle of the wheel is by far the largest. It is divided by spokes into six segments, each of which depicts what can be seen as a whole realm of existence – although these segments may alternatively be seen as representing a state of mind or plane of consciousness. The order varies, but always right at the top are the gods, who live in luxurious, elegant palaces and are surrounded by all manner of delights. For them existence is like a pleasant dream. Some of the gods have bodies made entirely of light, and they communicate by pure thought. Next, going round this circle in clockwise order, we see the *asuras* or 'jealous gods'. Clad in armour and wielding weapons, asuras live in a state of constant hostility and jealousy. They continually fight and compete for possession of the fruits of the 'wish-fulfilling tree'. In the next segment we see various species of animals: fish, insects, birds, reptiles, mammals. Some are large, some small, some are peaceful, some predatory, but all are searching for food. The bottom segment is a hellish realm full of tormented beings. Some are freezing in blocks of ice, others are burning in the flames, still others are being devoured by monsters. In the next segment up, on the left, we see the hungry ghosts. They have enormous swollen bellies but thin necks and mouths no larger than the eyes of tiny needles. All are ravenously hungry, but whatever food they touch turns either to fire or to filth. In the last segment, we see human beings among houses, fields, and gardens. Some people are cultivating the earth, while others are buying and selling, giving alms, or meditating.

These are the vividly contrasting six worlds, the six planes of consciousness, the six kinds of mental state depicted within the Tibetan Wheel of Life. It should be said, however, that the inhabitants of these worlds do not remain in them indefinitely. They disappear from one segment and reappear in another. Even the gods, although they stay a very long time in their world, eventually disappear and reappear somewhere else.

The outermost circle, the rim of the wheel, details the precise stages of the process by which living beings either pass from segment to segment of the previous circle, or else reappear in the same segment. Twelve stages are depicted, each arising in dependence on the previous one. In clock-wise order these are:

(1) a blind man with a stick – representing ignorance;

(2) a potter with a wheel and pots – representing volitional activities;

(3) a monkey climbing a flowering tree – representing sentience;

(4) a boat with four passengers, one of whom is steering – representing the psycho-physical organism;

(5) an empty house with five windows and a door – representing the six senses;

(6) a man and a woman embracing – representing contact;

(7) a man with an arrow in his eye – representing feeling;

(8) a woman offering a drink to a seated man – representing craving;

(9) a man gathering fruit from a tree – representing grasping;

(10) a pregnant woman – representing becoming, or life;

(11) a woman giving birth to a child – representing birth;

(12) a corpse being carried to the cremation ground – representing death and decay.

The wheel upon which all these images are ever revolving is clutched from behind by a fearful monster, half demon, half beast. His head, with its three eyes, long fangs, and crown of skulls, peers over the top, his clawed feet stick out either side, and his tail hangs down below.

But there is something more. Above the wheel to the right stands a figure in a yellow robe. This figure points to the space between the seventh and eighth segments of the outermost circle of the wheel, be-tween the man with the arrow in his eye and the woman who is offering a drink to a man. Here, rising out of this space, we see the second thing the Buddha saw in his vision of human existence. Again, it is not so much a symbol as a group of symbols, and it seems to change its form as we look at it.

At first there appears to be a path that stretches far away into the distance, winding now through cultivated fields, now through dense forest. It traverses swamps and deserts, broad rivers and deep ravines; it winds around the feet of mighty, cloud-capped mountains. Eventually, the path disappears over the horizon. But now the symbol changes. The path seems to straighten out, to stand up; it becomes a great ladder stretching from heaven to earth and from earth to heaven. It's a ladder of gold, a ladder of silver, a ladder of crystal. But again the symbol changes. The ladder becomes slender and solid and turns green; it becomes the stem of a gigantic tree with enormous blossoms, blossoms that are bigger the higher up they are. At the very top of the tree, shining like a sun, is the biggest blossom of all. In the centre of each of these blossoms sit all kinds of beautiful and radiant figures: Buddhas and Bodhisattvas, arhants, dakas and dakinis.

Such was the Buddha's vision of human existence as he sat beneath the bodhi tree – his vision as communicated in concept and symbol. The significance of the vision is quite clear. It is a vision of possibilities, of alternatives. On the one hand, we have cyclical conditionality, on the other, spiral conditionality. On the one hand, we have the reactive mind, on the other, the creative mind. We can either stagnate or grow. We can either continue to revolve passively and helplessly on the wheel, or we can follow the path, climb the ladder, become the plant, become the blossoms. Our fate is in our own hands.

Today the world is full of woolly thinking. Wrong views abound. They all in one way or another represent rationalizations of a limited range of experience. What we need today, perhaps more than anything else, is Right view – vision that is penetrating, unblinkered, and undistorted. We need the Perfect Vision communicated by the Buddha. If we have this vision, we can grow and develop. Without it, we may well perish. This is indeed a challenge that the Buddha lays before us, a challenge that has great implications for the way we live our lives. And those of us who take up this challenge will find ourselves forming the nucleus of a new society – the subject we will now move on to consider.

3

THE NUCLEUS OF A NEW SOCIETY

HERE MY PURPOSE IS TO MAKE CLEAR what Buddhism, and in particular the FWBO, has to offer, what it has to give – and this is only fitting since giving, or generosity, is of the very essence of the Dharma. We may even say that where there is no giving, there is no Buddhism. However, so far as the FWBO is concerned, the gifts offered so far are, to some extent at least, external to the FWBO itself. The gift and the giver are distinct. After all, other Buddhist organizations also offer these gifts – a method of personal development and a vision of human existence – albeit in different forms.

In the case of the third gift, by contrast, there is no distinction between the gift and the giver. I want to focus on the nucleus of a new society, and to explore the ways in which the FWBO *is* such a nucleus. In other words, one of the things the FWBO has to offer is itself. In his poem 'Song of Myself' Walt Whitman says, 'When I give, I give myself,' and this, we may say, is real giving. One can give many things – time, energy, money, ideas, work – and yet still not give the greatest of all gifts, oneself.

Since this third gift is of a different nature from the previous two, I want to present it differently. I want to start, in a way that some people would consider rather 'unbuddhistic', by saying something about myself, and how and why I came to start the Friends of the Western Buddhist Order and the Western Buddhist Order. I will then go on to outline what they are and in what way they form the nucleus of a new society.

Altogether I spent some twenty years in the East, including a year in Sri Lanka (which was then Ceylon), a year in Singapore, and eighteen years in India, as well as making visits to Nepal and Sikkim. During all that time I studied and practised Buddhism. However, I discovered Buddhism not in the East but in London, at the age of sixteen – or rather I should say that at sixteen I realized that I was already a Buddhist and had always been one. I made this discovery when I read two remarkable Buddhist texts: the *Diamond Sutra* and the *Sutra of Hui Neng*.

The *Diamond Sutra*, one of the shorter Perfection of Wisdom texts, is recited, meditated upon, and studied throughout the whole Buddhist world, particularly in countries that follow the Mahayana tradition, like China, Japan, and Tibet. Its content is too profound to be summed up in a few words. Suffice it to say that it deals with *shunyata*, with Ultimate Reality or, literally, the 'Void', and with the Wisdom that intuits the Void. The *Sutra of Hui Neng*, the 'Platform Scripture', is in a sense the basic text of the Ch'an, or Zen, tradition. It is a collection of discourses by – and dialogues and exchanges with – the great master Hui Neng (formerly rendered Wei Lang), the first Chinese patriarch of the Ch'an tradition. And again, it is pointless, indeed impossible, to offer any brief idea of its contents, if only because it goes beyond ideas – being, as it is, also concerned with fundamental reality. All I can say is that these two works gave me my first glimpse of the transcendental. Buddhist terminology refers to the transcendental as the *lokuttara*, which means 'beyond the world, the mundane, the conditioned'. In other words, these texts gave me my first glimpse of Perfect Vision. From then on I had no doubts about Buddhism, or about the spiritual path.

I did not meet any other Buddhists until I was eighteen. Consequently, for two years I was a Buddhist entirely on my own in a non-Buddhist world – in South London, to be precise – and when I say it was non-Buddhist I mean that Buddhism had virtually never been heard of in that world. In my nineteenth year I was conscripted into the Royal Corps of Signals and sent to India. This was in 1944. After the war ended I spent two years wandering mainly in South India, often on foot. For several years I lived like an Indian *sadhu* or ascetic. I wore saffron robes, carried a begging-bowl, and wandered barefoot from place to place, finding shelter under a tree, in a cave, or at some hospitable temple or ashram. And of course I met all sorts of people.

Eventually I settled in Kalimpong, a small town 4,000 feet above sea level in the eastern Himalayas. From where I lived there were stunning views of the snowy ranges, including the second highest peak in the Himalayas, Kanchenjunga, whose name means 'the Five Treasures of the Snow'. Except during the rainy season, one could see Kanchenjunga almost every day, its crest – wearing, very often, white plumes of snow blown off it by the wind – standing out against the blue sky with the clouds far below. The atmosphere was so clear that you could see for vast distances, and everything stood out with a strange, almost hypnotic, vividness of colour. Sometimes, especially just after the rains, the colours were so bright that everything seemed to be made of jewels – the brilliant white mountains, the intensely blue sky, the vivid green vegetation, the scarlet, yellow, and blue mountain flowers, and the gay, multicoloured costumes of the Tibetans, Bhutanese, Sikkimese, and Indian people.

I lived in this world of jewels for fourteen years. After seven years, I founded a small vihara, where people stayed with me from time to time. During this period I delved more and more deeply into the study and practice of Buddhism. Fortunately I made contact with quite a number of great teachers, especially some Tibetan teachers who were among those just beginning to come to India, and from them I received various ordinations and initiations. I also travelled to the cities of Calcutta, Bombay, and Delhi, as well as to Buddhist holy places like Bodh Gaya, Sarnath, Lumbini, Rajgir, and Nalanda. And during the second half of those fourteen years I also became involved in the mass conversion of ex-Untouchable Hindus to Buddhism.

In addition to studying and meditating, I spent a lot of time writing, especially during the rainy season, which in Kalimpong is a beautiful time of the year. The days are still warm, but the rain comes down all day and every day. You hear it falling peacefully on the roofs, on the leaves of the trees, and on the crops in the fields. Everything becomes quiet and hushed. Since there are no visitors, one can work, meditate, or write in peace. For a number of years the rainy season was my favourite time for writing.

While I lived in Kalimpong, I kept in touch with Buddhists in London through letters and Buddhist magazines, and it came to my notice towards the end of my time there (1962–3) that all was not well with the Buddhist movement in England, especially in London. Although it was a tiny movement, it had already divided into two opposing camps between which, to put it mildly, feelings ran high. Some of my friends felt that my presence in England, at least for a while, might help to restore harmony, and so towards the end of 1963 the English Sangha Trust invited me to England for a visit.

The invitation came as quite a surprise. Happily buried in my books and my meditation in Kalimpong, I took it for granted that I would continue my life in India and would die there. I never expected to see England again. But when the invitation arrived, I considered it long and deeply, and discussed it with my friends and teachers, and they all recommended that I should go. Some even felt it was my duty to go inasmuch as I might be able to restore harmony.

So in August 1964, after an absence of twenty years, I returned to England. I did not stay for the four months I originally planned, but for more than two years. I could not seem to get away. During that time I held meditation classes and gave many lectures, mainly at the Hampstead Buddhist Vihara in London, as well as at the premises of the Buddhist Society in Eccleston Square. In addition I visited a number of little – in many cases, tiny – Buddhist groups up and down the country.

Gradually it became clear that the Buddhist movement in England at that time left much to be desired. At the same time I saw that there were people in England who were greatly interested in the Dharma. After again deeply considering the situation and consulting with friends, I decided that I would stay and work for Buddhism in England and the West indefinitely. But first I needed to return to India for a few months and say goodbye to my teachers and friends, and turn over my responsibilities – especially for the vihara in Kalimpong.

I had not been back in India for more than a month when there came a bolt from the blue. I received a letter from the English Sangha Trust stating that it did not propose to renew its invitation and that I would no longer be welcome at the Hampstead Buddhist Vihara. The letter suggested that I should write a statement saying that I had changed my mind and would be staying in India after all; they offered to publish this letter for me in England.

When I read that letter I was standing in the Maha Bodhi Society's headquarters in Calcutta, about to make my way up to Kalimpong in the company of a friend. I remember that I passed the letter over to my friend to read, and said, 'Do you know what this means?' He said, 'No, what does it mean?' And I said, 'It means a new Buddhist movement.' Unbidden, in a flash, the idea for the FWBO had come upon me – as though I actually saw it looming, as it were, in the future.

Evidently during my two years in England I had unintentionally offended several people. Among other things I had succeeded in bringing together the two camps into which, at the time of my arrival, most English Buddhists were divided. This sudden unity had upset extremists on both sides, and they had joined forces to stop me from returning. I was warned – ludicrous as it may sound – that they were prepared to go to any lengths to stop me returning, and from the tone of alarm in some of my correspondence it seemed that I risked being murdered if I went back. Clearly I had trodden on some people's toes very heavily.

However, I did not hesitate. Only rarely in one's life does one find oneself in a position to make a completely free, uncomplicated choice, and I felt at that time that I was in that position. The alternatives were clear. On the one hand, I could remain in India, where I had been for eighteen years. I had founded a vihara in Kalimpong, I had many friends and teachers, I liked India very much, and I was quite happy there. It was a deeply, richly satisfying life. On the other hand, I could return to England, where I had nowhere to stay, no money, and no support from existing Buddhist organizations.

I made my choice, and I never doubted for a moment that it was the right one. Towards the end of March 1967 I returned to England for good. I wasn't murdered, and although I had been warned that I should find every door closed against me, this did not turn out to be the case – at least not entirely. I even found I had some friends left. A few weeks after my return, in April 1967, I started the FWBO.

It is perhaps still not completely clear from the foregoing history precisely why a new movement was needed. Before going on to outline the principal features of the FWBO I must first attempt to characterize the gap – or rather the gaping hole – in English Buddhism that needed to be filled. To begin with, many people who belonged to and controlled Buddhist organizations in England, including some of the people whom I had upset and who tried to prevent my return, were not actually Buddhists. Indeed, they did not even profess to be Buddhists. They had become members of Buddhist organizations simply by paying a subscription. Having joined in this fashion, they could be elected to office and thereby determine policy, even though they knew little or nothing about Buddhism and might even have had no real sympathy with it. This may sound strange, but it is by no means uncommon; indeed, the same thing went on in India. For example, the Maha Bodhi Society, with which I was associated, was virtually taken over by orthodox Hindus, whose ideas were quite opposed to those of Buddhism. It was therefore clear that we needed a new kind of Buddhist organization, one that could not be joined simply by paying a subscription. We needed an organization that one could join – if that is the word – only by committing oneself to the ideals for which it stood. In other words, we needed an Order and a spiritual community, or Sangha.

Other considerations also led me to this conclusion. As I have mentioned, the Buddhist movement in England at that time was barely alive. There were Buddhist societies and people who were interested in Buddhism, but only a few people were actually *practising* Buddhism. For example, most English Buddhists were not vegetarians, and few practised Right Livelihood or even thought of doing so. English Buddhists in those days lived the same kind of life – usually quite a middle-class life – as everybody else. Indeed, in those days many English Buddhists prided themselves on being just like everybody else. Personally I found this frustrating because I felt that people were not taking Buddhism seriously. They came to classes and lectures and came up to me afterwards to say how much they had enjoyed them, but then they carried on just as before. Nothing I said seemed to have any discernible effect on their lives. They did not change in any way – they did not even want to change. Clearly this state of affairs could not continue.

On my return to England in 1967, therefore, I decided to found an Order: a Western Buddhist Order. First, however, I founded the FWBO, the Friends of the Western Buddhist Order, and under its auspices I held meditation classes, gave lectures, organized retreats in the country, and so on. Gradually I gathered together two or three dozen people who took Buddhism seriously and wanted to change their lives. Some of these people I had known before, during my two-year preliminary visit; others were new. In April 1968 twelve of those people became the first members of the WBO, and the new Buddhist movement came into existence. From those modest beginnings that movement has grown until it now consists of many hundreds of Order members, of both sexes and all adult age groups, who live and work in many different countries in the West and, since the 1980s, in India (where the movement is not, for obvious reasons, called the FWBO, but TBMSG – Trailokya Bauddha Mahasangha Sahayak Gana).

So how does one join the Western Buddhist Order, if not by paying a subscription? And what is the relation between the WBO and the FWBO? To answer the first question first, one joins the Western Buddhist Order by Going for Refuge to the Three Jewels: the Buddha, the Enlightened Teacher; the Dharma, the teaching he gave; and the Sangha, all those who have attained transcendental insight through following the Buddha's path. The Buddha represents the ideal of human Enlightenment, and

Going for Refuge to the Buddha means committing oneself to the realiz-ation of that ideal, reorienting one's whole life in that direction. The Dharma represents the path leading to the realization of this ideal. It is in principle the sum total of all the methods and practices that help in one's personal development, in one's realization of the ideal. Thus Going for Refuge to the Dharma means actually practising the Dharma. The Sangha represents the spiritual community, the community of those who have gone for Refuge, who have committed themselves to the ideal of Enlightenment and who are practising the Dharma in order to reach that ideal. Going for Refuge to the Sangha means associating with such people, being in communication with them, learning from them, being inspired by them.

Going for Refuge is the central act of the Buddhist life. Going for Refuge to the Buddha, the Dharma, and the Sangha is what makes one a Buddh-ist. One could even go so far as to say that one's whole Buddhist life is, in a way, a progressive deepening of the Going for Refuge. And one goes for Refuge with one's entire self – with body, speech, and mind. It is not enough to think and feel that you are Going for Refuge. It is not enough even to *say* that you are. You must also *enact* the Going for Refuge; and when one joins the Western Buddhist Order this enactment takes place in a twofold ordination ceremony.

First there is a private ordination which one undertakes alone with a private preceptor – that is, one of a number of senior Order members designated to ordain people. One repeats after him – or her – the words of the Three Refuges: 'To the Buddha for Refuge I go; to the Dharma for Refuge I go; to the Sangha for Refuge I go.' At the same time one undertakes to observe the Ten Precepts of ethical behaviour. Three of these precepts refer to bodily actions, four to speech, and three to the mind. Together they represent the purification and transformation of one's entire being. At this private ordination ceremony one is also given a new name to signify that one is now spiritually reborn, having commit-ted oneself with body, speech, and mind to the Three Jewels.

The private ordination signifies your individual commitment to the Three Jewels – that is why it is a private ceremony. It signifies the fact that you have made up your mind to go for Refuge quite independently of any pressure or influence. You have made up your mind as an individual. You are in a state of mind in which you don't, in a sense, care if nobody else in the world is Going for Refuge. This is what *you* have made up your mind to do, and so you are going to do it. The private ordination signifies that sort of resolution – your determination, if it should ever be necessary, to go it alone.

Usually within a few days of the private ordination, the public ordination takes place, in the presence of other Order members (ideally at least five). Here too the words of the Going for Refuge are repeated, this time after a public preceptor, and the ordinand again undertakes to observe the Ten Precepts. On this occasion the new Order member is invested with a white *kesa*, a simple strip of material embroidered with an emblem of the Three Jewels and worn around the neck. The public ordination represents the fact that, although you are prepared to lead the spiritual life alone, you are not alone. You have become a member of a community of spiritually committed individuals, a member of the Order.

Originally the Western Buddhist Order was conceived of as a lay order rather than a monastic order, an Order in which people would commit themselves to the Three Jewels and work on their personal development within the framework of ordinary family life and a full-time job (one in accordance with Right Livelihood, of course). However, as time went on more and more Order members wanted to give a fuller expression to their commitment. They wanted to give as much as possible of their time and energy to the spiritual life and the work of the FWBO, and they found it difficult to do so within the framework of family life and a regular job. Consequently different roles developed for Order members. Today some Order members are married, some are unmarried, and some have taken a precept of celibacy. Some have full-time jobs, some have part-time jobs, and some have no regular jobs at all. The last usually work full time for the Dharma, and may receive living expenses from the FWBO. Some Order members live at home with their families, others live in communities of various kinds, and a few live on their own. Regardless of these differences, all these Order members are united by a common commitment to the Three Jewels. Thus it is no longer possible to call the Western Buddhist Order a lay order, any more than it can be called a monastic order. Perhaps it represents a new kind of development, one more in line with the original spirit of the Dharma.

As for the relation between the Order and the FWBO, we should be clear first of all that strictly speaking there is no such thing as the FWBO as a whole. There are only FWBOs: the FWBO, West London; the FWBO, Auckland; the FWBO, San Francisco; TBMSG, Bombay; and so on. All these FWBOs are autonomous; all run their own affairs. There is no centralization, no headquarters, and no organizational pyramid to hold them together. But spiritually they are held together by the Order inasmuch as each FWBO is run by Order members working co-operatively. Each FWBO has its own premises and plans its own particular programme of activities, such as meditation classes, yoga classes, lectures, study classes, retreats, arts events, and so on. Since the single purpose of all these activities is to help people in their personal development, they are variously designed to serve the spiritual needs of all who care to come along.

The various FWBOs represent, therefore, the means through which Order members offer their services, offer themselves, to society at large. Each FWBO is an autonomous registered charity (depending, that is, on the legal situation that obtains in any particular country). But the Order itself is a purely spiritual body. It is not a legal entity and therefore has no legal existence.

Not all Order members are occupied in running FWBOs, however. Some may for a long time devote themselves mainly to meditation, some may occupy themselves with literary work, or art or music, or study, while others may spend their time principally in raising their children, and still others may give themselves to travelling from place to place, visiting different FWBOs and making fresh contacts. But whatever they may be doing, the essential thing is that Order members keep in regular contact with one another by means of weekly and monthly meetings and biennial Order conventions, as well as in other ways and on other occasions.

Not all the FWBOs are urban centres running a regular programme of activities. Some function as country retreat centres. Others are residential communities of one kind or another. In certain cases groups of Order members may not function through an FWBO at all but rather through a different kind of organizational set-up, like a publishing house, a school, a restaurant, a housing association, or a business run in accordance with the principles of Right Livelihood, a topic we will explore in the next chapter.

As we have seen, people join the Order by Going for Refuge to the Three Jewels, by making a spiritual commitment to their personal development, alone as well as in spiritual fellowship with others who are also committed spiritually. However, except in very rare cases, this commitment does not happen the minute a person comes into contact with the Dharma and the FWBO. Usually people decide to commit themselves gradually, step by step. There may even be quite a struggle. Part of you wants to develop, part of you doesn't. For a while you may not even know whether you want to or not.

But suppose you come into contact with the FWBO – perhaps you see a poster, or perhaps a friend takes you – or drags you – to a talk or a meditation class. If you like it and you start coming regularly, you are considered a Friend with a capital 'F'. You have not joined anything – you are simply participating regularly. You don't have to believe or disbelieve in anything either. You can be a Christian, Jew, humanist, agnostic, free-thinker, spiritualist, occultist, Theosophist, Rosicrucian, Sufi, Vedantist – anything you like. This stage of being a Friend can last as long as you like. Many people, in fact, will not want to go any further than this.

If, however, you feel the need for a more definite link with Buddhism, with the Dharma, with the Order, you can ask to become a Mitra (the term is Sanskrit and means 'friend'). You become a Mitra – when you are considered to be ready by Order members who know you – by offering a flower, a candle, and a stick of incense in front of an image of the Buddha in the devotional context of a Sevenfold Puja, in the presence of Order members, Mitras, and Friends.

As is true for Order members, some Mitras live in communities, usually with Order members or other Mitras, while others live at home with their families or on their own. Some Mitras and Friends have jobs, whereas others work full- or part-time for the FWBO. There are special activities – study groups, retreats, and so on – commensurate in intensity with their level of commitment. But again, you can stay a Mitra for as long as you like. If you do want to deepen your involvement, the next step is to ask for ordination. There are special retreats for those preparing themselves to make this full commitment to the Three Jewels. The time it takes for each person to become ready for ordination varies very much because for each person it is a very individual process.

As I have explained how one may become more deeply involved with the FWBO, and how one may avail oneself of what it has to offer, I hope that the way in which the FWBO is the nucleus of a new society has become clear. As you become first a Friend, then a Mitra, then an Order member, you become more of an individual. That is, you become more aware, more sensitive, more responsible, more emotionally positive, more at home in higher states of consciousness, and you have an increasingly clearer and deeper vision of human existence. In other words, you develop spiritually. Furthermore, the more you become an individual yourself, the more you relate to others as an individual, and on the basis of common spiritual ideals. Within the context of the Order this means relating to other Order members more and more on the basis of a common spiritual commitment to the Three Jewels.

Usually, unfortunately, we do not relate to other people as individuals. We tend to relate to people as members of a particular group, profession, nationality, race, sex, age group, income bracket, political party, trade union, and so on. We relate to others on the basis of competition or conflict, or else common need, whether this be economic, political, psychological, or sexual. There is thus the possibility of two kinds of society: on the one hand, a society of individuals based on common spiritual ideals and a common commitment to personal development; and on the other, a society of non-individuals who are simply members of various groups. The first I would term a spiritual community, and the second a 'group'. The first type of society is what I am choosing to call the new society; the second is the old society. The first is based on the spiral type of conditionality, the second on the cyclical type. The first is the achievement of the creative mind, the second the product of the reactive mind. Finally, of course, the first is very small, the second very large. But although it is a daunting task, we must try nevertheless to turn the second into the first, to transform the group into the spiritual community, the old society into the new. I want to move on to discuss some of the ways in which this transformation can be achieved.

It is as the nucleus of a new society that the FWBO offers itself, a nucleus of which the Order is the central and most essential part. The FWBO offers itself not as an organization but as a spiritual community that is willing to welcome into spiritual fellowship all those who want to grow and develop.

4

A BLUEPRINT FOR A NEW WORLD

THUS FAR, WE HAVE DEALT WITH THINGS that are immediately available, things that are laid out all ready for us to experience. We have them here and now. Not just one method of personal development but a whole range of methods already exist, and people are actually using them and benefiting from them. Similarly there is a vision of human existence, the vision seen by the Buddha and his Enlightened disciples, which we can all glimpse, at least occasionally. And the nucleus of a new society exists quite concretely in the form of the FWBO.

Looked at in this way, a blueprint for a new world is a quite different subject inasmuch as that new world does not exist yet. If it exists at all it exists only in the imagination, only as a dream. But it is no less worthy of our attention for that. The imagination, after all, has its uses. What we imagine today we may do tomorrow; the dream of the night may become the reality of the morning. Let us imagine, let us dream, and we may find that we are closer to reality than we had thought.

Whether a new world seems to us like a distant dream or an approaching reality, most of us will probably think that a 'blueprint for a new world' sounds like a good idea. As any advertising copywriter will tell you, we all respond with approval to the word 'new'. There are of course other words we find attractive. I had a friend once who specialized in publishing popular books on 'the wisdom of the East' and he used to say that if he wasn't very sure of the quality of a book he was bringing out, he would insist that the word 'secret' should be inserted in the title – as in 'The Secret Teachings of....' The blueprint I am referring to makes no such claims as this. It is not a 'secret blueprint'. But it *is* a blueprint for something new – for a new world – and we may find the idea attractive.

If we do find the idea of a new world attractive, this is presumably for the same reason that we find the idea of anything new attractive: because we are not really satisfied with the old model. However, when we say that we are dissatisfied with the old world, what exactly do we mean? Are we dissatisfied with the earth, with the flowers or the trees? Well, no. When we say that we are dissatisfied with the world, we generally mean that we are dissatisfied with certain aspects of corporate human existence, with certain social, economic, and political arrangements, even with the quality of human life. We are all of us, in one way or another, dissatisfied with the world in this sense. The real question to ask ourselves is: are we dissatisfied enough? Does our dissatisfaction go deep enough? Or is it like the motorist's dissatisfaction with his or her car? Yes, one would like a quieter and more powerful engine, power-assisted steering, air bags, more leg-room in the back, and so on. But to what extent is one dissatisfied with that mode of transport as such? To what extent is one really dissatisfied with polluting the air with exhaust fumes or with a way of life that obliges one to spend hours hunched over the wheel instead of walking?

We may be dissatisfied with the amount of money we earn, but our dissatisfaction does not extend so readily to the very idea of working for a wage. We may be dissatisfied with our personal relationships, but do we ever get round to being dissatisfied with the emotional dependence on which those relationships are usually based? We tend to be more dissatisfied with the economic and political status of the country we belong to than we are with nationalism and the whole concept of the sovereign national state. We may be dissatisfied with wars and conflicts all over the globe, but not with those things for which people go to war.

What I'm suggesting is that we do not really want a new world at all; we only want an improved version, perhaps merely a slightly improved version, of the old world. The world that I have in mind, however, is an entirely new world, a world radically different from the old one. This new world will be a world in which we relate to one another as individuals, a world in which we are free to develop to the utmost of our potential, and in which the social, economic, and political structures will help us to do that. The new world will be, in short, a spiritual community – a spiritual community writ large. Our aim, therefore, must be to transform the present world into a spiritual community. This is the only new world that is worth having, the only new world worth working for.

But how are we to bring about this transformation? How are we even to begin? First of all, we must reconcile two apparently divergent views as to how best to go about instituting the kind of radical change I am envisaging. The first view says we must change the system. People are basically all right as they are; they are simply unlucky enough to live under the wrong system. All we need to do, therefore, is replace the wrong system with the right one, and we shall then have a new world in which everybody will be happy. The second view says that change must come from the bottom up; that it is simply up to the individual, as the basic unit of society, to change. Those who hold this view may go so far as to think that the individual human being is greedy, selfish, and stupid, and that all the world's troubles are due to this simple fact. Wars occur because people feel hatred, economic crises occur because people are greedy. It follows that to change the world we must change ourselves: we must become contented, unselfish, generous, and wise. The first view, that we must change the system, is generally regarded as the secular view, and the second, which is a sort of moral appeal – sometimes a vehement moral appeal – to the ordinary individual, is generally regarded as the spiritual view.

In fact these views are not mutually exclusive. Spiritual movements, especially those that trace their descent from 'the wisdom of the East', are generally expected to adopt the spiritual view, but if this is so, the FWBO is an exception. Yes, the development of the individual is fundamental in transforming the world; but at the same time it is important to recognize that external conditions can help or hinder us in our development. Whatever the external conditions, we have to want to develop and we will always have to exert ourselves. But we must also acknowledge that if we live under the right system, it is easier to develop, and if we live under the wrong system, it is more difficult.

Having said that, some people depend less on external conditions than others; in other words, some are more truly individual than others. There are those who will develop no matter how unfavourable the external conditions may be; they will somehow find a way through despite all obstacles. Others, by contrast, will find it almost impossible to develop even if conditions are highly favourable, while still others, of course, simply won't be interested in development at all. But for most people external conditions are important. With the right conditions they will develop, and with the wrong conditions they will not. It's as simple as that.

This becomes clear on a retreat. A retreat involves a number of people going to a beautiful, quiet place in the country for a weekend, or a week, or a month (retreats come in all shapes and sizes). Except for taking turns at cooking, washing dishes, or perhaps some gardening, the participants do not work. Instead they meditate perhaps three or four times a day, they chant together, they take part in pujas, they listen to talks, and they have discussions or study Buddhist texts. In other words, for a time the conditions under which people live are changed; they are provided with conditions that are more conducive to personal development. And in these improved conditions, people change. One can see this happening literally before one's eyes. Sometimes people change dramatically, even after just a few days. They might arrive on the retreat feeling worried, harried, anxious, tired, and irritable – but gradually they become more relaxed, they cheer up, they begin to smile and laugh and seem glad to be alive. They become more aware of themselves, of one another, of their surroundings, of nature, more aware that they are living and breathing on this earth. They also become more free and spontaneous, more themselves. Although I have seen this happen many times, each time the change occurs it seems almost magical.

Unfortunately, however, the retreat must end, and everyone has to go back to wherever they came from. And it is noticeable that people who have experienced a retreat for the first time can be quite reluctant to leave. They can even become tearful at the prospect of going back to less helpful conditions. Indeed, because we generally have to return to a boring or otherwise stressful job, to a noisy crowded city, or to a difficult domestic situation, the change in us does not always last. Nevertheless there is one lasting benefit: we have seen that it is possible to change, that – given the right conditions – we can develop.

It is, therefore, not altogether true after all to say that to offer a blueprint for a new world is to dream of something that does not exist. On retreat we experience, at least to a small extent and for a short time, what the new world could be like. We can even say that on a small scale a retreat *is* a new world. It shows us that the idea of transforming the world into a spiritual community is more than a mere hypothesis. It shows us that the new world need not exist only in the imagination; it is not just a dream.

So, to come back to our original question, how do we go about transforming the world into a spiritual community? How do we begin? Usually people who want to change the world do two things. First they draw up a detailed, comprehensive plan, and then they try to get everybody to adopt it – by force if necessary. Of course some people choose to do only one of these two things. Either they think it is enough to create the plan and leave others to accept it or reject it as they wish, or else they try to seize power in the conviction that once they attain it they will know what to do with it.

From the Buddhist point of view neither of these two courses of action is satisfactory. To begin with, Buddhists distrust abstract theories, theories not directly related to the needs of the concrete human situation. Buddhism delineates general principles but leaves the specific application of those principles to the individual. Take ethics, for example. Buddhism teaches the principle of non-violence, or love, and says that we should do no harm to other living beings. It teaches the principle of generosity and says that we should not take what is not given. In both cases Buddhist tradition indicates some of the more obvious applications of these principles, but it leaves us to understand and enact the principles within the context of our own lives. It is the same in connection with the projection of an ideal world. Buddhist texts describe such a world, but the descriptions are general and inspirational rather than specific; again, we are left to work out the details for ourselves.

As for changing the world by first seizing power and only then developing a plan for an ideal society, this sort of scheme, pragmatic as it may be, is even less suited to Buddhist principles. The spiritual community is not a power structure. It is not based on coercion, or on the authority of one person over another. The spiritual community cannot be created by the exercise of power; only persuasion, through words or through personal example, can bring it into existence. Otherwise, the new world would only be a variant of the old one, with all the old problems.

So what are we to do? The answer is really quite simple. If we want to build a new world, we must expand the nucleus of a new society into the old world. This expansion represents the activity of the spiritual community; it is not just the individual actions of individual committed Buddhists, but rather the actions of *teams* of committed Buddhists. Such teamwork can radically transform two fundamental aspects of our lives: what we do to earn a living, and where we live.

Almost all of us have to work. Right Livelihood, therefore, is an integral part of spiritual life and personal development, so integral that it is the fifth element of the Buddha's Noble Eightfold Path. Right Livelihood consists in earning a living without doing harm – whether physical, psychological, ethical, or spiritual – to any living being, including yourself. Ideally, the way in which you earn a living should help yourself and others to grow, directly or indirectly. Even in the world as it is, under existing conditions, we should be able to practise Right Livelihood, especially if we are not trying to earn as much money as possible as quickly as possible, if we are prepared to live simply. This will certainly help the individual to grow and develop, especially if he or she is determined and self-sufficient. However, it will not necessarily help to bring a new world into existence. For this, we need teams of committed Buddhists – in the case of the FWBO, teams of Order members, Mitras, and Friends – practising Right Livelihood collectively.

It is possible to set up business organizations in much the same way that FWBO centres are founded: a team of people decide to pool their talents, energy, and resources, and work together to create a new venture. What type of business a team sets up is determined by the principles of Right Livelihood; profits are ploughed back into the business or used to subsidize other FWBO activities.

This type of arrangement has many advantages. First of all, the team members involved are provided with a means of Right Livelihood. They do not receive a salary, but are given whatever they need to cover their living expenses. This might mean that the work would in some circumstances be shared among a larger number of people than would be usual in the outside world, in order that team members might devote sufficient time to meditation, study, or the arts.

Secondly, Order members, Mitras, and Friends work together on the basis of a common spiritual commitment. One of the best ways of learning to communicate with and relate to people is by working with them. In a team-based Right Livelihood business the team members not only practise Right Livelihood, which is in itself a spiritual practice; they work with other spiritually committed people, which is also a spiritual practice.

Thirdly, the business aims to produce something that is of positive value to society at large. It may be something quite basic like food or clothing, or something of cultural value like books and magazines, or else a service like the repair and decoration of houses, or catering, or even schools or nursing homes.

Fourthly, the business should ideally earn money to support and extend Buddhist activities and facilities that produce little or no income.

Right Livelihood businesses may finance special events or the establishment of Buddhist centres. In a society in which the general public is largely indifferent to Buddhist ideals, Right Livelihood enterprises represent one way of raising the necessary funds. Here again, with Right Livelihood, the blueprint has got well beyond the drawing board and is embodied in a wide range of thriving businesses, which are all realizing the aims and ideals of team-based Right Livelihood with greater or lesser success.

There is just one more thing that should be mentioned with respect to Right Livelihood businesses. As we have seen, the Western Buddhist Order is not a monastic community in the traditional sense. It is not a community of monks, or *bhikkhus* – a term that literally means 'those who live on alms'. According to the old tradition, the bhikkhu goes once a day from door to door and collects cooked food. He does not need even to cook it, let alone grow it or earn the money to pay for it. He accepts clothing and shelter wherever he can find them. This means that he can lead a very simple life. He has no need to work. Since he depends directly on the lay public for food, clothing, and shelter, he is free to devote all his time to meditation, study, teaching, or writing. As I related in the last chapter, I have myself had some experience of this way of life. Such a life is possible in India because most people believe in the spiritual values according to which the monk lives, even though they do not themselves attempt to live up to those values to anything like the same extent. People are therefore happy to support the monk, believing that they also benefit by doing this.

Needless to say, it is not possible to be a bhikkhu in most Western countries; it is not possible to depend directly on the general public for alms. In fact, if you tried to beg for food from door to door, you might even be arrested. In the West most people set little store by spiritual values, and the law reflects this fact. Unfortunately, the same state of affairs is beginning to develop in India. Notices are now appearing outside villages in northern India saying that *sadhus* – that is ascetics, holy men, or monks – who beg will be prosecuted. In some modern, 'progressive' quarters in India, monks are simply considered to be economically non-productive.

So what is the Buddhist monk in the West to do? Although I have translated the term *bhikkhu* as 'one who depends on alms', it can also be interpreted to mean 'one who shares' – that is, one who shares in the common wealth, who is supported out of the surplus that society produces. This, in the FWBO, is where Right Livelihood businesses come in.

If businesses produce a profit, they are then able not only to provide Right Livelihood for the team members involved but also to support those Order members who are devoting the whole of their time to meditation, study, and so on. Such Order members will in effect be monks, at least from the economic point of view. They will not depend on the general public but rather on the FWBO, on other individuals who share the same spiritual ideals. This arrangement is already operating on a small scale. A good many Order members are supported by the FWBO and devote all their time and energy to the work of the FWBO and to their own spiritual practice. Such Order members form the heart of the movement. They may not be wearing yellow robes, but in certain important respects they live like monks. The fact that such monks depend not on the general public but on the movement suggests that the FWBO is itself a society, a society within the larger society, a small world within the greater world.

Whether or not it is the case that we all have to work, it is certainly the case that we all have to live somewhere. Of course, the most usual living situation has always been, and continues to be, the family – although what this means in Western society today is very different from what it used to mean. The family used to include not only parents and children but unmarried aunts, grandparents, distant cousins, plus various dependants – what we would call an 'extended family'. Although people still live like this in some parts of the world, especially in the East, in modern Western countries families tend to be much smaller – so small, in fact, as to be almost claustrophobic. The scope for personal relations within this tiny family group is limited, and the relationships that do exist tend to be emotionally overloaded, and so tend to produce psychological tensions that can explode with destructive and disintegrating effects.

As an alternative to these small, overloaded, claustrophobic groups, many people practising Buddhism in the context of the FWBO are choosing to live in residential communities based on devotion to a common spiritual ideal. In these communities, Order members, Mitras, and Friends live together on the basis of a common commitment to the Three Jewels and to spiritual development. Today there are many such residential communities throughout the world, and they represent a particular kind of collective presence in the world – indeed, a particular aspect of the new world.

Residential spiritual communities are as varied as the individuals who live in them. Some are in towns, some in cities, and some in the countryside. In the early days of the FWBO some communities included both men and women, with or without children, but these days by far the majority of communities consist of either men or women. Experience has shown that single-sex communities are the most effective and supportive context for spiritual practice.

The advantages of living in a community are quite clear. You can enjoy the regular companionship of other spiritually committed people. You are free to relate at the deepest level of your being, which is very stimulating and inspiring – and also challenging and demanding. You can live economically, since community members can pool resources and buy food in bulk, share the use of things like refrigerators, cars, and washing machines, and also share household chores and child care, if there are children in the community. And spiritual communities also function as a kind of informal Buddhist centre: members can give friends and visitors a glimpse of a new way of life. .

Through Right Livelihood businesses and communities, as well as in many other ways, the Western Buddhist Order is expanding into the world. The new world starts with individuals, but not just with individuals on their own. It starts with spiritually committed teams of individuals. These teams create situations that help people grow, situations that correspond to people's needs, whether economic, artistic, or social. Together, indeed, the various structures created constitute, on a small scale, a new world. So we already have a detailed blueprint for a new world, or something that is perhaps even better: the living, growing seed of a new world. The acorn is the real blueprint for the oak tree.

Although I have covered a lot of ground very briefly, I hope that I have managed at least to convey these four things: a method of personal development to be practised, a vision of human existence to provide inspiration, the nucleus of a new society to be enjoyed, and a blueprint of a new world to be worked for. These four things are what the FWBO has to offer the modern man and woman – a Buddhism for today and tomorrow.

•

Recommended Reading

A Method of Personal Development

On evolution:

Robin Cooper (Ratnaprabha), *The Evolving Mind*, Windhorse, Birmingham 1996.

Sangharakshita, *Mind – Reactive and Creative*, Windhorse, Birmingham 1995.

Sangharakshita, *Human Enlightenment*, Windhorse, Glasgow 1993.

Sangharakshita, *The FWBO and 'Protestant Buddhism'*, Windhorse, Glasgow 1992. See the chapter 'Modernism and Buddhism' p.75.

Sangharakshita, *The Priceless Jewel*, Windhorse, Glasgow 1993. See the essay 'The Bodhisattva Principle', p.137.

On meditation:

Kamalashila, *Meditation: The Buddhist Way of Tranquillity and Insight*, Windhorse, Glasgow 1992.

A Vision of Human Existence

Sangharakshita, *Vision and Transformation*, Windhorse, Glasgow 1990, see chapter 1: 'Perfect Vision'.

Sangharakshita, *The Meaning of Conversion in Buddhism*, Windhorse, Birmingham 1994.
Subhuti, *The Buddhist Vision*, Rider, London 1985.
On the Wheel of Life and conditionality:
Sangharakshita, *A Guide to the Buddhist Path*, Windhorse, Glasgow 1990.
Sangharakshita, *The Three Jewels*, Windhorse, Glasgow 1991.
Sangharakshita, *The Buddha's Victory*, Windhorse, Glasgow 1991.

The Nucleus of a New Society

Subhuti, *Buddhism for Today*, Windhorse, Glasgow 1988.
Sangharakshita, *New Currents in Western Buddhism*, Windhorse, Glasgow 1990.
On Sangharakshita's life:
Subhuti, *Bringing Buddhism to the West*, Windhorse, Birmingham 1995.
Sangharakshita, *The Thousand-Petalled Lotus*, Alan Sutton, Gloucester 1988.
Sangharakshita, *Facing Mount Kanchenjunga*, Windhorse, Glasgow 1991.

A Blueprint For a New World

Subhuti, *Sangharakshita: A New Voice in the Buddhist Tradition*, Windhorse, Birmingham 1995, chapter 9.
Sangharakshita, *Transforming Self and World*, Windhorse, Birmingham 1995.
Sangharakshita, *The Inconceivable Emancipation*, Windhorse, Birmingham 1995.
On the Diamond Sutra:
Sangharakshita, *Wisdom Beyond Words*, Windhorse, Glasgow 1993, part 3.

•

INDEX

The Windhorse symbolizes the energy of the enlightened mind carrying the Three Jewels
– the Buddha, the Dharma, and the Sangha – to all sentient beings.
Buddhism is one of the fastest growing spiritual traditions in the Western world.
Throughout its 2,500-year history, it has always succeeded in adapting its mode of
expression to suit whatever culture it has encountered.
Windhorse Publications aims to continue this tradition as Buddhism comes to the West.
Today's Westerners are heirs to the entire Buddhist tradition, free to draw instruction and
inspiration from all the many schools and branches. Windhorse publishes works by
authors who not only understand the Buddhist tradition but are also familiar with
Western culture and the Western mind.

For orders and catalogues contact

WINDHORSE PUBLICATIONS

UNIT 1-316 THE CUSTARD FACTORY

GIBB STREET

BIRMINGHAM

B9 4AA

UK

WINDHORSE PUBLICATIONS (USA)

14 HEARTWOOD CIRCLE

NEWMARKET

NEW HAMPSHIRE

NH 03857

USA

Windhorse Publications is an arm of the Friends of the Western Buddhist Order, which has more than sixty centres on four continents. Through these centres, members of the Western Buddhist Order offer regular programmes of events for the general public and for more experienced students. These include meditation classes, public talks, study on Buddhist themes and texts, and 'bodywork' classes such as t'ai chi, yoga, and massage. The FWBO also runs several retreat centres and the Karuna Trust, a fundraising charity that supports social welfare projects in the slums and villages of India.

Many FWBO centres have residential spiritual communities and ethical businesses associated with them. Arts activities are encouraged too, as is the development of strong bonds of friendship between people who share the same ideals. In this way the FWBO is developing a unique approach to Buddhism, not simply as a set of techniques, less still as an exotic cultural interest, but as a creatively directed way of life for people living in the modern world.

If you would like more information about the FWBO please write to

LONDON BUDDHIST CENTRE

51 ROMAN ROAD

LONDON

E2 OHU

UK

ARYALOKA

HEARTWOOD CIRCLE

NEWMARKET

NEW HAMPSHIRE

NH 03857

USA